# STRATEGY TO COMBAT TRANSNATIONAL ORGANIZED CRIME

## Addressing Converging
## Threats to National Security

JULY 2011

**Transnational organized crime** refers to those self-perpetuating associations of individuals who operate transnationally for the purpose of obtaining power, influence, monetary and/or commercial gains, wholly or in part by illegal means, while protecting their activities through a pattern of corruption and/or violence, or while protecting their illegal activities through a transnational organizational structure and the exploitation of transnational commerce or communication mechanisms. There is no single structure under which transnational organized criminals operate; they vary from hierarchies to clans, networks, and cells, and may evolve to other structures. The crimes they commit also vary. Transnational organized criminals act conspiratorially in their criminal activities and possess certain characteristics which may include, but are not limited to:

- In at least part of their activities they commit violence or other acts which are likely to intimidate, or make actual or implicit threats to do so;

- They exploit differences between countries to further their objectives, enriching their organization, expanding its power, and/or avoiding detection/apprehension;

- They attempt to gain influence in government, politics, and commerce through corrupt as well as legitimate means;

- They have economic gain as their primary goal, not only from patently illegal activities but also from investment in legitimate businesses; and

- They attempt to insulate both their leadership and membership from detection, sanction, and/or prosecution through their organizational structure.

July 19, 2011

In the National Security Strategy, I committed my Administration to the pursuit of four enduring national interests: security, prosperity, respect for universal values, and the shaping of an international order that can meet the challenges of the 21st century. The expanding size, scope, and influence of transnational organized crime and its impact on U.S. and international security and governance represent one of the most significant of those challenges.

During the past 15 years, technological innovation and globalization have proven to be an overwhelming force for good. However, transnational criminal organizations have taken advantage of our increasingly interconnected world to expand their illicit enterprises.

Criminal networks are not only expanding their operations, but they are also diversifying their activities, resulting in a convergence of transnational threats that has evolved to become more complex, volatile, and destabilizing. These networks also threaten U.S. interests by forging alliances with corrupt elements of national governments and using the power and influence of those elements to further their criminal activities. In some cases, national governments exploit these relationships to further their interests to the detriment of the United States.

Despite a long and successful history of dismantling criminal organizations and developing common international standards for cooperation against transnational organized crime, not all of our capabilities have kept pace with the expansion of 21st century transnational criminal threats. Therefore, this strategy is organized around a single, unifying principle: to build, balance, and integrate the tools of American power to combat transnational organized crime and related threats to our national security – and to urge our partners to do the same. To this end, this strategy sets out 56 priority actions, starting with ones the United States can take within its own borders to lessen the impact of transnational crime domestically and on our foreign partners. Other actions seek to enhance our intelligence, protect the financial system and strategic markets, strengthen interdiction, investigations, and prosecutions, disrupt the drug trade and its facilitation of other transnational threats, and build international cooperation.

While this Strategy is intended to assist the United States Government in combating transnational crime, it also serves as an invitation for enhanced international cooperation. We encourage our partners and allies to echo the commitment we have made here and join in building a new framework for international cooperation to protect all our citizens from the violence, harm, and exploitation wrought by transnational organized crime.

Sincerely,

# Table of Contents

# Executive Summary

The *Strategy to Combat Transnational Organized Crime* applies all elements of national power to protect citizens and U.S. national security interests from the convergence of 21<sup>st</sup> century transnational criminal threats. This *Strategy* is organized around a single unifying principle: *to build, balance, and integrate the tools of American power to combat transnational organized crime and related threats to national security—and to urge our foreign partners to do the same.* The end-state we seek is to reduce transnational organized crime (TOC) from a national security threat to a manageable public safety problem in the United States and in strategic regions around the world. The *Strategy* will achieve this end-state by pursuing five key policy objectives:

1. Protect Americans and our partners from the harm, violence, and exploitation of transnational criminal networks.

2. Help partner countries strengthen governance and transparency, break the corruptive power of transnational criminal networks, and sever state-crime alliances.

3. Break the economic power of transnational criminal networks and protect strategic markets and the U.S. financial system from TOC penetration and abuse.

4. Defeat transnational criminal networks that pose the greatest threat to national security by targeting their infrastructures, depriving them of their enabling means, and preventing the criminal facilitation of terrorist activities.

5. Build international consensus, multilateral cooperation, and public-private partnerships to defeat transnational organized crime.

The *Strategy* also introduces new and innovative capabilities and tools, which will be accomplished by prioritizing within the resources available to affected departments and agencies.

A new Executive Order will establish a sanctions program to block the property of and prohibit transactions with significant transnational criminal networks that threaten national security, foreign policy, or economic interests.

A proposed legislative package will enhance the authorities available to investigate, interdict, and prosecute the activities of top transnational criminal networks.

A new Presidential Proclamation under the Immigration and Nationality Act (INA) will deny entry to transnational criminal aliens and others who have been targeted for financial sanctions.

A new rewards program will replicate the success of narcotics rewards programs in obtaining information that leads to the arrest and conviction of the leaders of transnational criminal organizations that pose the greatest threats to national security.

An interagency Threat Mitigation Working Group will identify those TOC networks that present a sufficiently high national security risk and will ensure the coordination of all elements of national power to combat them.

# I. Introduction

*"Combating transnational criminal and trafficking networks requires a multidimensional strategy that safeguards citizens, breaks the financial strength of criminal and terrorist networks, disrupts illicit trafficking networks, defeats transnational criminal organizations, fights government corruption, strengthens the rule of law, bolsters judicial systems, and improves transparency. While these are major challenges, the United States will be able to devise and execute a collective strategy with other nations facing the same threats."*

— *National Security Strategy*, May 2010

In January 2010, the United States Government completed a comprehensive review of international organized crime—the first on this topic since 1995. Based on the review and subsequent reporting, the Administration has concluded that, in the intervening years, international —or transnational— organized crime has expanded dramatically in size, scope, and influence and that it poses a significant threat to national and international security. In light of the review's findings, we have adopted the term "transnational organized crime" (TOC) to describe the threats addressed by this *Strategy*. While the term "international organized crime" has been commonly used in the past, "transnational organized crime" more accurately describes the converging threats we face today. As emphasized in the *National Security Strategy*: "…these threats cross borders and undermine the stability of nations, subverting government institutions through corruption and harming citizens worldwide."

In years past, TOC was largely regional in scope, hierarchically structured, and had only occasional links to terrorism. Today's criminal networks are fluid, striking new alliances with other networks around the world and engaging in a wide range of illicit activities, including cybercrime and providing support for terrorism. Virtually every transnational criminal organization and its enterprises are connected and enabled by information systems technologies, making cybercrime a substantially more important concern. TOC threatens U.S. interests by taking advantage of failed states or contested spaces; forging alliances with corrupt foreign government officials and some foreign intelligence services; destabilizing political, financial, and security institutions in fragile states; undermining competition in world strategic markets; using cyber technologies and other methods to perpetrate sophisticated frauds; creating the potential for the transfer of weapons of mass destruction (WMD) to terrorists; and expanding narco-trafficking and human and weapons smuggling networks. Terrorists and insurgents increasingly are turning to criminal networks to generate funding and acquire logistical support. TOC also threatens the interconnected trading, transportation, and transactional systems that move people and commerce throughout the global economy and across our borders.

In October 2010, the national security advisors of 44 nations gathered in Sochi, Russia to discuss transnational crime. Representing the United States, former National Security Advisor General James L. Jones, USMC, Ret. warned of the TOC threats to international security and urged immediate international action, saying:

*"In a world full of transnational threats, transnational crime is in an ascendant phase… This lethal nexus of organized crime, narco-trafficking, and terrorism is a threat that the United States, Russia and all of us share and should be working together to combat… Today, right now, we have an opportunity for cooperation not just between the United States and Russia, but among all nations represented here today. It's up to us to seize the moment…"*

The various elements of this *Strategy* flow from a single unifying principle: we will *build, balance, and integrate the tools of American power to combat TOC and related threats to national security and urge our foreign partners to do the same.* To this end, the *Strategy* recognizes TOC as a significant threat to national and international security and emphasizes U.S. planning, priorities, and activities accordingly. The *Strategy* addresses TOC and drug trafficking as increasingly intertwined threats to maximize the impact of U.S. resources. It also provides a framework to direct U.S. power against those TOC actors, activities, and networks that are determined to pose the greatest threat to national and international security.

This *Strategy* establishes priority actions in several key areas. It starts by taking a hard look at what actions the United States can take within its own borders to lessen the threat and impact of TOC domestically and on our foreign partners. The other priority actions seek to:

- Enhance Intelligence and Information Sharing;

- Protect the Financial System and Strategic Markets Against Transnational Organized Crime;

- Strengthen Interdiction, Investigations, and Prosecutions;

- Disrupt Drug Trafficking and Its Facilitation of Other Transnational Threats; and

- Build International Capacity, Cooperation, and Partnerships.

This *Strategy* complements but does not replicate the work of other major U.S. security initiatives. It is guided by the *National Security Strategy* and interlocks with other U.S. strategies and initiatives, to include the *National Drug Control Strategy*, the *National Strategy for Counterterrorism*, the *International Strategy for Cyberspace*, the *National Strategy to Combat Weapons of Mass Destruction*, the U.S.-Mexico *Merida Initiative*, the *Law Enforcement Strategy to Combat International Organized Crime*, the *National Strategy for Maritime Security, Countering Piracy Off the Horn of Africa: Partnership & Action Plan*, and several other U.S. security assistance, counterdrug, and capacity-building efforts around the world.

The Interagency Policy Committee (IPC) on Illicit Drugs and Transnational Criminal Threats will oversee a whole-of-government approach to implementing this *Strategy*. Co-chaired by the National Security Staff and the Office of National Drug Control Policy, this IPC will issue implementation guidance, establish performance measures, and receive regular progress updates from the interagency community. This IPC will be informed by and work with other IPCs such as the Maritime Security IPC. With a new *Strategy to Combat Transnational Organized Crime* and an array of new authorities and tools, this Administration is committing itself to ensuring that we rise to the national security challenges of the 21st century and ensure an international order that protects the safety and well-being of our citizens.

# II. Transnational Organized Crime: A Growing Threat to National and International Security

Transnational organized crime (TOC) poses a significant and growing threat to national and international security, with dire implications for public safety, public health, democratic institutions, and economic stability across the globe. Not only are criminal networks expanding, but they also are diversifying their activities, resulting in the convergence of threats that were once distinct and today have explosive and destabilizing effects. This *Strategy* organizes the United States to combat TOC networks that pose a strategic threat to Americans and to U.S. interests in key regions.

**Penetration of State Institutions, Corruption, and Threats to Governance.** Developing countries with weak rule of law can be particularly susceptible to TOC penetration. TOC penetration of states is deepening, leading to co-option in a few cases and further weakening of governance in many others. The apparent growing nexus in some states among TOC groups and elements of government—including intelligence services—and high-level business figures represents a significant threat to economic growth and democratic institutions. In countries with weak governance, there are corrupt officials who turn a blind eye to TOC activity. TOC networks insinuate themselves into the political process in a variety of ways. This is often accomplished through direct bribery (but also by having members run for office); setting up shadow economies; infiltrating financial and security sectors through coercion or corruption; and positioning themselves as alternate providers of governance, security, services, and livelihoods. As they expand, TOC networks may threaten stability and undermine free markets as they build alliances with political leaders, financial institutions, law enforcement, foreign intelligence, and security agencies. TOC penetration of governments is exacerbating corruption and undermining governance, rule of law, judicial systems, free press, democratic institution-building, and transparency. Further, events in Somalia have shown how criminal control of territory and piracy ransoms generate significant sums of illicit revenue and promote the spread of government instability.

**Threats to the Economy, U.S. Competitiveness, and Strategic Markets.** TOC threatens U.S. economic interests and can cause significant damage to the world financial system through its subversion, exploitation, and distortion of legitimate markets and economic activity. U.S. business leaders worry that U.S. firms are being put at a competitive disadvantage by TOC and corruption, particularly in emerging markets where many perceive that rule of law is less reliable. The World Bank estimates about $1 trillion is spent each year to bribe public officials, causing an array of economic distortions and damage to legitimate economic activity. The price of doing business in countries affected by TOC is also rising as companies budget for additional security costs, adversely impacting foreign direct investment in many parts of the world. TOC activities can lead to disruption of the global supply chain, which in turn diminishes economic competitiveness and impacts the ability of U.S. industry and transportation sectors to be resilient in the face of such disruption. Further, transnational criminal organizations, leveraging their relationships with state-owned entities, industries, or state-allied actors, could gain influence over key commodities markets such as gas, oil, aluminum, and precious metals, along with potential exploitation of the transportation sector.

**Crime-Terror-Insurgency Nexus.** Terrorists and insurgents increasingly are turning to TOC to generate funding and acquire logistical support to carry out their violent acts. The Department of Justice reports that 29 of the 63 organizations on its FY 2010 Consolidated Priority Organization Targets list, which includes the most significant international drug trafficking organizations (DTOs) threatening the United States, were associated with terrorist groups. Involvement in the drug trade by the Taliban and the Revolutionary Armed Forces of Colombia (FARC) is critical to the ability of these groups to fund terrorist activity. We are concerned about Hizballah's drug and criminal activities, as well as indications of links between al-Qa`ida in the Lands of the Islamic Maghreb and the drug trade. Further, the terrorist organization al-Shabaab has engaged in criminal activities such as kidnapping for ransom and extortion, and may derive limited fees from extortion or protection of pirates to generate funding for its operations. While the crime-terror nexus is still mostly opportunistic, this nexus is critical nonetheless, especially if it were to involve the successful criminal transfer of WMD material to terrorists or their penetration of human smuggling networks as a means for terrorists to enter the United States.

**Expansion of Drug Trafficking.** Despite demonstrable counterdrug successes in recent years, particularly against the cocaine trade, illicit drugs remain a serious threat to the health, safety, security, and financial well-being of Americans. The demand for illicit drugs, both in the United States and abroad, fuels the power, impunity, and violence of criminal organizations around the globe. Mexican DTOs are escalating their violence to consolidate their market share within the Western Hemisphere, protect their operations in Mexico, and expand their reach into the United States. In West Africa, Latin American cartels are exploiting local criminal organizations to move cocaine to Western Europe and the Middle East. There have also been instances of Afghan DTOs operating with those in West Africa to smuggle heroin to Europe and the United States. Many of the well-established organized criminal groups that had not been involved in drug trafficking—including those in Russia, China, Italy, and the Balkans—are now establishing ties to drug producers to develop their own distribution networks and markets. The expansion of drug trafficking is often accompanied by dramatic increases in local crime and corruption, as the United Nations has detected in regions such as West Africa and Central America.

*With the expansion of the drug trade, illicit drugs have become more lethal over the years. The number of Americans who died each year from accidental overdoses from all drugs, but mostly illicit ones, more than tripled from 1992 to 2007, increasing to 38,000.*

**Human Smuggling.** Human smuggling is the facilitation, transportation, attempted transportation, or illegal entry of a person or persons across an international border, in violation of one or more countries' laws, either clandestinely or through deception, whether with the use of fraudulent documents or through the evasion of legitimate border controls. It is a criminal commercial transaction between willing parties who go their separate ways once they have procured illegal entry into a country. The vast majority of people who are assisted in illegally entering the United States and other countries are smuggled, rather than trafficked. International human smuggling networks are linked to other transnational crimes including drug trafficking and the corruption of government officials. They can move criminals, fugitives, terrorists, and trafficking victims, as well as economic migrants. They undermine the sovereignty of nations and often endanger the lives of those being smuggled. In its 2010 report *The Globalization of Crime: A Transnational Organized Crime Threat Assessment,* the United Nations Office on Drugs and Crime (UNODC) estimated that the smuggling of persons from Latin America to the United States generated approximately $6.6 billion annually in illicit proceeds for human smuggling networks.

Trafficking in Persons. Trafficking in Persons (TIP), or human trafficking, refers to activities involved when one person obtains or holds another person in compelled service, such as involuntary servitude, slavery, debt bondage, and forced labor. TIP specifically targets the trafficked person as an object of criminal exploitation—often for labor exploitation or sexual exploitation purposes—and trafficking victims are frequently physically and emotionally abused. Although TIP is generally thought of as an international crime that involves the crossing of borders, TIP victims can also be trafficked within their own countries. Traffickers can move victims between locations within the same country and often sell them to other trafficking organizations.

Weapons Trafficking. Criminal networks and illicit arms dealers also play important roles in the black markets from which terrorists and drug traffickers procure some of their weapons. As detailed in the 2010 UNODC report *The Globalization of Crime,* "The value of the documented global authorized trade in firearms has been estimated at approximately $1.58 billion in 2006, with unrecorded but licit transactions making up another $100 million or so. The most commonly cited estimate for the size of the illicit market is 10% - 20% of the licit market." According to the head of UNODC, these "illicit arms fuel the violence that undermines security, development and justice" worldwide. U.S. Federal law enforcement agencies have intercepted large numbers of weapons or related items being smuggled to China, Russia, Mexico, the Philippines, Somalia, Turkmenistan, and Yemen in the last year alone.

Intellectual Property Theft. TOC networks are engaged in the theft of critical U.S. intellectual property, including through intrusions into corporate and proprietary computer networks. Theft of intellectual property ranges from movies, music, and video games to imitations of popular and trusted brand names, to proprietary designs of high-tech devices and manufacturing processes. This intellectual property theft causes significant business losses, erodes U.S. competitiveness in the world marketplace, and in many cases threatens public health and safety. Between FY 2003 and FY 2010, the yearly domestic value of customs seizures at U.S. port and mail facilities related to intellectual property right (IPR) violations leaped from $94 million to $188 million. Products originating in China accounted for 66% of these IPR seizures in FY 2010.

Cybercrime. TOC networks are increasingly involved in cybercrime, which costs consumers billions of dollars annually, threatens sensitive corporate and government computer networks, and undermines worldwide confidence in the international financial system. Through cybercrime, transnational criminal organizations pose a significant threat to financial and trust systems—banking, stock markets, e-currency, and value and credit card services—on which the world economy depends. For example, some estimates indicate that online frauds perpetrated by Central European cybercrime networks have defrauded U.S. citizens or entities of approximately $1 billion in a single year. According to the U.S. Secret Service, which investigates cybercrimes through its 31 Electronic Crimes Task Forces, financial crimes facilitated by anonymous online criminal fora result in billions of dollars in losses to the Nation's financial infrastructure. The National Cyber Investigative Joint Task Force, led by the Federal Bureau of Investigation (FBI), functions as a domestic focal point for 18 federal departments or agencies to coordinate, integrate, and share information related to cyber threat investigations, as well as make the Internet safer by pursuing terrorists, spies, and criminals who seek to exploit U.S. systems. Pervasive criminal activity in cyberspace not only directly affects its victims, but can imperil citizens' and businesses' faith in these digital systems, which are critical to our society and economy. Computers and the Internet play a role in most transnational crimes today, either as the target or the weapon used in the crime. The use of the Internet, personal computers, and mobile devices all create a trail of digital evidence. Often the proper investigation of this evidence trail requires highly trained personnel. Crimes can occur more quickly, but investigations proceed more slowly due to the critical shortage of investigators with the knowledge and expertise to analyze ever increasing amounts of potential digital evidence.

The Critical Role of Facilitators. Connecting these converging threats are "facilitators," semi-legitimate players such as accountants, attorneys, notaries, bankers, and real estate brokers, who cross both the licit and illicit worlds and provide services to legitimate customers, criminals, and terrorists alike. The range of licit-illicit relationships is broad. At one end, criminals draw on the public reputations of licit actors to maintain facades of propriety for their operations. At the other end are "specialists" with skills or resources who have been completely subsumed into the criminal networks. For example, TOC networks rely on industry experts, both witting and unwitting, to facilitate corrupt transactions and to create the necessary infrastructure to pursue their illicit schemes, such as creating shell corporations, opening offshore bank accounts in the shell corporation's name, and creating front businesses for their illegal activity and money laundering. Business owners or bankers are enlisted to launder money, and employees of legitimate companies are used to conceal smuggling operations. Human smugglers, human traffickers, arms traffickers, drug traffickers, terrorists, and other criminals depend on secure transportation networks and safe locations from which to stage smuggling activity or to store bulk cash or narcotics for transport. They also depend on fraudulently created or fraudulently obtained documents, such as passports and visas, to move themselves or their clients into the United States and illegally reside here.

Transnational criminal networks such as organized crime groups, drug traffickers, and weapons dealers at times share convergence points—places, businesses, or people—to "launder" or convert their illicit profits into legitimate funds. Many of these disparate networks also appear to use the same casinos, financial intermediaries, and front companies to plan arms and narcotics deals because they view them as safe intermediaries for doing business. Cash-intensive and high-volume businesses such as casinos are especially attractive, particularly those in jurisdictions that lack the political will and oversight to regulate casino operations or fail to perform due diligence on casino licensees. Illicit networks similarly abuse some of the same financial intermediaries and front companies in regions where government or law enforcement corruption is prevalent, with officials receiving either revenues from the criminal businesses or ownership stakes in the legitimate-appearing commercial entity.

## Regional Priorities

*TOC—a global problem—manifests itself in various regions in different ways.*

**Western Hemisphere:** TOC networks—including transnational gangs—have expanded and matured, threatening the security of citizens and the stability of governments throughout the region, with direct security implications for the United States. Central America is a key area of converging threats where illicit trafficking in drugs, people, and weapons—as well as other revenue streams— fuel increased instability. Transnational crime and its accompanying violence are threatening the prosperity of some Central American states and can cost up to eight percent of their gross domestic product, according to the World Bank. The

Mexico Los Zetas Cartel Leaders Heriberto Lazcano-Lazcano and Miguel Angel Treviño Morales

Government of Mexico is waging an historic campaign against transnational criminal organizations, many of which are expanding beyond drug trafficking into human smuggling and trafficking, weapons smuggling, bulk cash smuggling, extortion, and kidnapping for ransom. TOC in Mexico makes the U.S. border more vulnerable because it creates and maintains illicit corridors for border crossings that can be employed by other secondary criminal or terrorist actors or organizations. Farther south, Colombia has achieved remarkable success in reducing cocaine production and countering illegal armed groups, such as the FARC, that engage in TOC. Yet, with the decline of these organizations, new groups are emerging such as criminal bands known in Spanish as *Bandas Criminales,* or *Bacrims.*

---

### Colombia: From Recipient to Provider of Assistance

After years of intensive capacity building assistance in Colombia, the United States is working to transfer financial and operational responsibility for institutional development to the Government of Colombia. Colombia now is an exporter of law enforcement and justice sector capabilities, providing assistance and advice for police, prosecutors, protection programs, and judiciary, criminal law, and procedure development. This reality is the result of the success of U.S. assistance in Colombian capacity building, a success the United States aims to replicate with other partner states. On July 2, 2008, the world witnessed the extraordinary courage and capability of Colombian forces during their daring rescue of 15 hostages—including 3 Americans—who had been held captive for years in the jungles by FARC guerrillas. The rescue was accomplished without firing a shot.

---

**Afghanistan/Southwest Asia:** Nowhere is the convergence of transnational threats more apparent than in Afghanistan and Southwest Asia. The Taliban and other drug-funded terrorist groups threaten the efforts of the Islamic Republic of Afghanistan, the United States, and other international partners to build a peaceful and democratic future for that nation. The insurgency is seen in some areas of Afghanistan as criminally driven—as opposed to ideologically motivated—and in some areas, according to local Afghan officials and U.S. estimates, drug traffickers and the Taliban are becoming indistinguishable. In other instances, ideologically

INTERPOL Fugitive Dawood Ibrahim, South Asia "Company D"

driven insurgent networks are either directly trafficking in narcotics or have linked up with DTOs to finance their criminal actions. The threatening crime-terror-insurgency nexus in this region is illustrated by cases such as that of INTERPOL fugitive Dawood Ibrahim, the reputed leader of South Asia's powerful "D Company." He is wanted in connection with the 1993 Mumbai bombing and is sanctioned under United Nations Security Council Resolution 1267 (Taliban/al-Qa`ida).

Russia/Eurasia: Russian and Eurasian organized crime networks represent a significant threat to economic growth and democratic institutions. Russian organized crime syndicates and criminally linked oligarchs may attempt to collude with state or state-allied actors to undermine competition in strategic markets such as gas, oil, aluminum, and precious metals. At the same time, TOC networks in the region are establishing new ties to global drug trafficking networks. Nuclear material trafficking is an especially prominent concern in the former Soviet Union. The United States will continue to cooperate with Russia and the nations of the region to combat illicit drugs and TOC.

The Balkans: A traditional conduit for smuggling between east and west, the Balkans has become an ideal environment for the cultivation and expansion of TOC. Weak institutions in Albania, Kosovo, and Bosnia and Herzegovina have enabled Balkan-based TOC groups to seize control of key drug and human trafficking routes and Western European markets. The Balkans region has become a new entry point for Latin American cocaine, a source of synthetic drugs, and a transit region for heroin chemical precursors for use in the Caucasus and Afghanistan. Excess weapons are smuggled to countries of concern. Insufficient border controls and the ease of acquiring passports enable the transit of criminals and terrorist figures to Western Europe. Cooperation between the United States and the European Union, as well as bilateral cooperation with the countries in the region to foster legal institution building, economic progress, and good governance in the Balkans will be key to eliminating the environment supporting TOC.

West Africa: West Africa has become a major transit point for illegal drug shipments to Europe and for Southwest Asian heroin to the United States. It has also become both a source of—and transit point for—methamphetamine destined for the Far East. West Africa also serves as a transit route for illicit proceeds flowing back to source countries. TOC exacerbates corruption and undermines the rule of law, democratic processes, and transparent business practices in several African states that already suffer from weak institutions. Due to its lack of law enforcement capabilities, its susceptibility to corruption, its porous borders, and its strategic

Jose Americo Bubo Na Tchuto, U.S. Treasury-designated drug kingpin

location, Guinea-Bissau remains a significant hub of narcotics trafficking on the verge of developing into a narco-state. While many officials within the Government of Guinea-Bissau recognize the extent of the drug problem and express a willingness to address it, a crippling lack of resources and capacity remains a hindrance to real progress in combating drug trafficking. The recent re-appointment of U.S. Treasury-designated drug kingpin Jose Americo Bubo Na Tchuto as Naval Chief of Staff is likely to further entrench drug cartels in the permissive operating conditions prevailing in Guinea-Bissau. In the Gulf of Guinea, maritime criminals operate in areas of weak governance, kidnapping oil workers, stealing oil from pipelines, and causing environmental damage that harms the citizenry. The United States will work with African governments, European partners, and multilateral institutions to counter this threat to development, democratic processes, and the rule of law in the region.

Asia/Pacific: TOC networks and DTOs are integrating their activities in the Asia/Pacific region. Due to the region's global economic ties, these criminal activities have serious implications worldwide. The economic importance of the region also heightens the threat posed to intellectual property rights, as a large portion of intellectual property theft originates from China and Southeast Asia. Human trafficking and smuggling remain significant concerns in the Asia/Pacific region, as demonstrated by the case of convicted alien smuggler Cheng Chui Ping, who smuggled more than 1,000 aliens into the United States during the course of her criminal career, sometimes hundreds at a time. TOC networks in the region are also active in the illegal drug trade, trafficking precursor chemicals for use in illicit drug production. North Korean government entities have likely maintained ties with established crime networks, including those that produce counterfeit U.S. currency, threatening the global integrity of the U.S. dollar. It is unclear whether these links persist. The United States will continue to improve its understanding of the TOC threats in the Asia/Pacific region and will work with partner nations to develop a comprehensive response.

Cheng Chui Ping, convicted alien smuggler

# III. Strategy to Combat Transnational Organized Crime

For decades, the United States and other countries have dismantled scores of criminal organizations around the world. The U.S. experience with La Cosa Nostra, as well as Colombia's experience with the Medellin and Cali Cartels—and even the FARC—prove that it is possible to constrain, shrink, disrupt and dismantle criminal and insurgent groups once considered to be untouchable.

This *Strategy* builds upon such past experience. Today the threat from TOC is more complicated because criminal networks are more fluid and are using increasingly sophisticated tactics. TOC can exploit the interconnected nature of our modern trading, transportation, and transactional systems that move people and commerce throughout the global economy and across our borders. Countering TOC today requires an integrated and comprehensive approach. This *Strategy* sets out such an approach to *raise international awareness* about the reality of the TOC threat to international security; *galvanize* multilateral action to *constrain* the reach and influence of TOC; *deprive* TOC of its enabling means and infrastructure; *shrink* the threat TOC poses to citizen safety, national security, and governance; and *ultimately defeat* the TOC networks that pose the greatest threat to national security. TOC presents sophisticated and multi-faceted threats that cannot be addressed through law enforcement action alone. Accordingly, we will establish an interagency Threat Mitigation Working Group to identify those TOC networks that present a sufficiently high national security threat as to merit the focused use of complementary law enforcement and non-law enforcement assets and that may be vulnerable to whole-of-government responses. The Working Group will ensure the coordination of all elements of national power to effectively protect our borders, people, economy, and financial system from the threats posed by the most dangerous and sophisticated of these transnational criminal networks.

This *Strategy* sets out five overarching policy objectives that are consistent with the vision and priorities of the *National Security Strategy*:

1. **Protect Americans and our partners from the harm, violence, and exploitation of transnational criminal networks.** Our priority is the safety, security, and prosperity of American citizens and the citizens of partner nations. We will target the networks that pose the gravest threat to citizen safety and security, including those that traffic illicit drugs, arms, and people—especially women and children; sell and distribute substandard, tainted and counterfeit goods; rob Americans of their prosperity; carry out kidnappings for ransom and extortion; and seek to terrorize and intimidate through acts of torture and murder.

2. **Help partner countries strengthen governance and transparency, break the corruptive power of transnational criminal networks, and sever state-crime alliances.** The United States needs willing, reliable and capable partners to combat the corruption and instability generated by TOC and related threats to governance. We will help international partners develop the sustainable capacities necessary to defeat transnational threats; strengthen legitimate and effective public safety, security, and justice institutions; and promote universal values. We will also seek to sever

STRATEGY TO COMBAT TRANSNATIONAL ORGANIZED CRIME

the powerful strategic alliances that form between TOC and states, including those between TOC networks and foreign intelligence services.

3.  Break the economic power of transnational criminal networks and protect strategic markets and the U.S. financial system from TOC penetration and abuse. TOC networks—using bribery, fraud, and violence—have the capacity to disrupt economic activity and put legitimate businesses at a distinct competitive disadvantage. We will attack the financial underpinnings of the top transnational criminals; strip them of their illicit wealth; sever their access to the financial system; expose their criminal activities hidden behind legitimate fronts; and protect strategic markets and the U.S. financial system.

4.  Defeat transnational criminal networks that pose the greatest threat to national security, by targeting their infrastructures, depriving them of their enabling means, and preventing the criminal facilitation of terrorist activities. We will target, disrupt, and defeat the TOC networks that pose the greatest threat to the safety and security of Americans and U.S. national security interests. These include criminal networks—including transnational criminal gangs—that traffic drugs, bulk cash, arms, people, sensitive documents, or other contraband. Further, we will seek to prevent collaboration between criminal and terrorist networks and deprive them of their critical resources and infrastructure, such as funding, logistical support for transportation, staging, procurement, safe havens for illicit activities, and the facilitation of services and materiel, which could include WMD material.

5.  Build international consensus, multilateral cooperation, and public-private partnerships to defeat transnational organized crime. We will build new partnerships—with industry, finance, academia, civil society and non-governmental organizations—to combat TOC networks that operate in the illicit and licit worlds. We will also fight criminal networks with an alliance of legitimate networks, and ensure the freedom of the press so that the media and journalists may safely expose the harms inflicted by TOC. We will expand and deepen our understanding, cooperation, and information sharing at home with State and local agencies, with foreign partners, and with multilateral institutions. Internationally, we will further international norms against tolerating or sponsoring crime in all its forms, including in cyberspace.

# Priority Actions

## Start at Home: Taking Shared Responsibility for Transnational Organized Crime

*I reiterated that the United States accepts our shared responsibility for the drug violence. So to combat the southbound flow of guns and money, we are screening all southbound rail cargo, seizing many more guns bound for Mexico, and we are putting more gunrunners behind bars. And as part of our new drug control strategy, we are focused on reducing the demand for drugs through education, prevention and treatment... We are very mindful that the battle President Calderón is fighting inside of Mexico is not just his battle; it's also ours. We have to take responsibility just as he's taking responsibility.*

—President Barack Obama speaking at a joint press conference
with Mexican President Felipe Calderón, March 3, 2011

We must begin our effort to disrupt TOC by looking inward and acknowledging the causes that emanate from within our own borders to fuel and empower TOC. The demand for illegal drugs within the United States fuels a significant share of the global drug trade, which is a primary funding source for TOC networks and a key source of revenue for some terrorist and insurgent networks. Any comprehensive strategy to defeat TOC must seek to reduce the demand for drugs and other illegal goods that finance TOC networks. The President's *National Drug Control Strategy* emphasizes prevention, early intervention, treatment, and innovative criminal justice approaches to drive down drug use, and calls for continued support for the millions of Americans who are in recovery from addiction. Supported by a budget that increases resources for vital prevention and treatment programs, the *National Drug Control Strategy* seeks to reduce the size of the illegal drug market in the United States, depriving TOC networks of revenue while helping more of our citizens break the cycle of drug abuse and reducing the adverse consequences to our communities.

We must also stop the illicit flow from the United States of weapons and criminal proceeds that empower TOC networks. The Administration has placed an increased emphasis on stemming these outbound flows, dedicating additional law enforcement, investigative, and prosecution resources to targeting TOC, such as deploying additional U.S. Customs and Border Protection "outbound teams" to our borders, screening outbound rail and vehicle traffic for weapons and bulk currency, and by investing additional resources in the integrated Border Enforcement Security Task Forces along the U.S.-Mexico border to investigate the organizations involved in cross-border crimes. We will also work with Congress to seek ratification or accession to key multilateral instruments related to countering the illicit trafficking of weapons.

Further, we will work with our international partners to build their law enforcement capacities, strengthen their judicial institutions, and combat the corrosive threat of corruption, while also recognizing that the United States itself is not immune to public corruption. Continued vigilance is required to ensure the integrity of U.S. officials and institutions as we face the new and converging threats posed by TOC. In addition to the greater vigilance required by our governmental institutions, American businesses and individuals need to inform law enforcement about criminal activity and reduce their vulnerability to fraud schemes, intellectual property theft, and identity theft. Acknowledging our own challenges and aggressively addressing them here at home represent the first essential steps in building the cooperative multilateral approach required to defeat TOC.

### Actions

A.  Reduce the demand for illicit drugs in the United States, thereby denying funding to illicit trafficking organizations.

B.  Continue to attack drug trafficking and distribution networks and their enabling means within the United States to reduce the availability of illicit drugs.

C.  Sever the illicit flow across U.S. borders of people, weapons, currency, and other illicit finance through investigations and prosecutions of key TOC leadership, as well as through the targeting of TOC networks' enabling means and infrastructure.

D.  Identify and take action against corporate and governmental corruption within the United States.

E.  Work with Congress to secure ratification of the Inter American Convention against the Illicit Manufacturing of and Trafficking in Firearms, Ammunition, Explosives and Other Related Materials.

F.  Seek accession to the Protocol against the Illicit Manufacturing of and Trafficking in Firearms, their Parts and Components and Ammunition, supplementing the UN Convention against Transnational Organized Crime.

---

**Project Deliverance: Targeting Mexican Drug Trafficking Networks in the United States**

On June 9, 2010 the DEA-led interagency Special Operations Division executed a coordinated takedown in support of Project Deliverance, a 22-month multi-agency network of law enforcement investigations targeting the transportation infrastructure of Mexican transnational criminal organizations in the United States, especially along the Southwest border. During the final takedown, 429 arrests took place in 16 states through coordination among more than 3,000 Federal, State, and local law enforcement officers. In total, Project Deliverance has led to 2,266 arrests and the seizure of $154 million, 1,262 pounds of meth-amphetamine, 2 5 tons of cocaine, 1,410 pounds of heroin, 69 tons of marijuana, 501 weapons, and 527 vehicles during the entire course of the operation.

---

## Enhance Intelligence and Information Sharing

A shift in U.S. intelligence collection priorities since the September 11, 2001 attacks left significant gaps in TOC-related intelligence. Meanwhile, the TOC threat has worsened and grown in complexity over the past 15 years. The fluid nature of TOC networks, which includes the use of criminal facilitators, makes targeting TOC increasingly difficult.

Enhancing U.S. intelligence collection, analysis, and counterintelligence on TOC is a necessary first step, but should be accompanied by collaboration with law enforcement authorities at Federal, State, local, tribal, and territorial levels and enhanced sharing with foreign counterparts. We will also supplement our understanding of TOC involvement in licit commercial sectors to better enable policymakers to develop specific interventions. Our aim is enhanced intelligence that is broad-based and centered on substantially upgraded signals intelligence (SIGINT), human intelligence (HUMINT) and open sources intelligence (OSINT). This effort will be aided through greater information sharing with foreign partners and closer cooperation among intelligence, law enforcement, and other applicable agencies domestically.

We will augment our intelligence in step with the new TOC threats described previously. The Administration will review its current intelligence priorities, including the National Intelligence Priorities Framework, and determine how best to enhance our intelligence against the highest-level TOC threats to national security. Priorities will include:

- Enhancing SIGINT and HUMINT collection on TOC threats, especially taking into account the potential role of TOC to facilitate WMD terrorism;

- Employing the Open Source Center to draw upon "grey" literature, smaller press outlets that cover crime in foreign countries, and social media fora to develop profiles of individuals, companies, and institutions linked to TOC networks;

- Coordinating with the interagency International Organized Crime Intelligence and Operations Center (IOC-2) to utilize existing resources and databases of the Organized Crime Drug Enforcement Task Force (OCDETF) Fusion Center (OFC) and SOD to share intelligence, de-conflict operations, and produce actionable leads for investigators and prosecutors working nationwide;

- Expanding collection and immigration, customs, transportation, and critical infrastructure screening capabilities in TOC "hotspots" around the world;

- Developing protocols to ensure appropriate TOC data flows to agencies conducting screening and interdiction operations to disrupt TOC activities at the border and at critical points of the supply chain;

- Using specialized intelligence centers such as the El Paso Intelligence Center, the Bulk Cash Smuggling Center, the National Export Enforcement Coordination Center, and the Cyber Crimes Center to coordinate the collection and analysis of intelligence regarding various aspects of the TOC threat;

- Using the National Intellectual Property Rights Coordination Center, an interagency and international law enforcement task force established in 2000 and led by ICE, to assist with combating intellectual property theft and maintaining the integrity of public health, public safety, the military, and the U.S. economy; and

- Enhancing Department of Defense support to U.S. law enforcement through the Narcotics and Transnational Crime Support Center.

## Actions

A. Enhance U.S. intelligence collection, analysis, and counterintelligence on TOC entities that pose the greatest threat to national security.

B. Develop greater synergies between intelligence analysts, collectors, and counterintelligence personnel; ensure their efforts directly support operational law enforcement needs and screening requirements.

C. Strengthen ties among U.S. intelligence and counterintelligence, law enforcement, and military entities, while strengthening cooperation with international intelligence and law enforcement partners.

D. Develop and foster stronger law enforcement and Intelligence Community relationships among Federal, State, local, tribal, and territorial authorities.

E. Support multilateral senior law enforcement exchanges to promote the sharing of criminal intelligence and enhance cooperation, such as the "Quintet of Attorneys-General" and the "Strategic Alliance Group" fora established with the United Kingdom, Canada, New Zealand, and Australia.

F. Update the National Intelligence Priorities Framework to ensure that it is aligned with current TOC threats.

G. Enhance support to Intelligence Community analysis of TOC by the Office of the Director of National Intelligence, specifically by the National Intelligence Council and the National Intelligence Managers.

H. The National Counterproliferation Center shall develop a plan that assesses the links between TOC and WMD proliferators.

I. Establish a comprehensive and proactive information-sharing mechanism to identify TOC actors and exclude them from the United States or uncover them within the United States.

---

### INFORMATION SHARING TO COMBAT TRANSNATIONAL ORGANIZED CRIME

**The Special Operations Division**

Established in 1994, the Special Operations Division (SOD) is a DEA-led multi-agency operations coordination center with participation from Federal law enforcement agencies, the Department of Defense, the Intelligence Community, and international law enforcement partners. SOD's mission is to establish strategies and operations to dismantle national and international trafficking organizations by attacking their command and control communications. Special emphasis is placed on those major drug trafficking and narco-terrorism organizations that operate across jurisdictional boundaries on a regional, national, and international level. SOD provides foreign- and domestic-based law enforcement agents with timely investigative information that enables them to fully exploit Federal law enforcement's investigative authority under Title III of the U.S. Code. SOD coordinates overlapping investigations, ensuring that tactical and operational intelligence is shared among law enforcement agencies.

### The Organized Crime Drug Enforcement Task Force Fusion Center

Created in June 2006, the Organized Crime Drug Enforcement Task Force (OCDETF) Fusion Center (OFC) serves as a central data warehouse for drug intelligence, financial intelligence, and related investigative information, and is designed to conduct cross-agency integration and analysis of such data with a view to creating comprehensive intelligence pictures of targeted organizations, including those identified as Consolidated Priority Organization Targets—the United States' most wanted international drug and money laundering targets. The OFC provides agencies with operational human and financial intelligence, and is staffed with agents and analysts detailed from 14 participating investigative agencies. These personnel conduct analysis to produce investigative leads, develop target profiles, and identify links between drug organizations and other criminal activity in support of drug investigations.

### The International Organized Crime Intelligence and Operations Center

In May 2009, Attorney General Eric Holder announced the establishment of the International Organized Crime Intelligence and Operations Center (IOC-2), an entity that marshals the resources and information of U.S. law enforcement agencies and Federal prosecutors to collectively combat the threats posed by international criminal organizations. Understanding that international criminal organizations are profit-driven, IOC-2 also works with investigators and prosecutors to target the criminal proceeds and assets of international criminal organizations. In recognition of the demonstrated interrelationship between criminal organizations that engage in illicit drug trafficking and those that engage in international organized crime involving a broader range of criminal activity, IOC-2 works in close partnership with the OFC and SOD.

### The Bulk Cash Smuggling Center

ICE established the National Bulk Cash Smuggling Center (BCSC) in 2009 to combat bulk cash smuggling. The BCSC is an operations support facility providing real-time investigative assistance to the Federal, State, and local officers involved in enforcement and interdiction of bulk cash smuggling and the transportation of illicit proceeds. The BCSC is partnered with the El Paso Intelligence Center to further identify and target the financial infrastructure of drug trafficking organizations. These organizations seek to avoid traditional financial institutions by repatriating illicit proceeds through commercial and private aircraft, passenger and commercial vehicles, maritime vessels, and pedestrians crossing at our U S. land borders. These combined interagency efforts, successful financial investigations, Bank Secrecy Act requirements, and anti-money laundering compliance by financial institutions has strengthened formal financial systems and forced criminal organizations to seek other means to transport illicit funds across our borders.

### The EPIC Border Intelligence Fusion Section

The El Paso Intelligence Center (EPIC), managed by the DEA, was established in 1974 to support enforcement efforts against drug and alien smuggling along the Southwest border. EPIC has grown over time to better support Federal, State, local and tribal law enforcement. The DHS Office of Intelligence and Analysis established the Border Intelligence Fusion Section (BIFS) at EPIC in November 2010 with the objective of providing U.S. law enforcement, border enforcement, and investigative agencies with multi-source intelligence and law enforcement information to support investigations, interdictions, and other law enforcement operations related to the Southwest border. The BIFS is a joint, collaborative effort of the Department of Homeland Security, Department of Justice, Department of Defense, and partners in the Intelligence Community and, as a multi-source/all threats intelligence section at EPIC, the BIFS will access and analyze intelligence and information received by and developed at EPIC in order to produce a common intelligence picture and common operating picture.

## Protect the Financial System and Strategic Markets Against Transnational Organized Crime

Transnational criminals are now more entrepreneurial and sophisticated, and their growing infiltration of licit commerce and economic activity fundamentally threatens the free markets and financial systems that are critical to the stability and efficiency of the global economy. TOC threatens free markets because it disregards the laws and norms that legitimate businesses respect, thereby reaping an unfair competitive advantage. By eroding market integrity, quality, and competitiveness and using financial systems to move, conceal, and increase illicit funds, transnational criminals exploit and undermine not only the interests of the United States but also those of all countries promoting the rule of law.

By carefully following strategic and emerging markets for indicators of criminal interest, the United States can detect, disrupt, and reduce the economic power of TOC. To do so, the United States will work with our international partners to deter or sever crime-state alliances, raise awareness to alert businesses that may be unwitting facilitators for criminal enterprises, and continue to develop appropriate safeguards to protect the legitimate flow of trade and investment. By targeting criminal assets and opportunities, the United States and its allies can markedly reduce the profitability, growth, and evolution of TOC networks.

However, some TOC activity is inherently harder to detect and deter. The United States will place special emphasis on IPR violations and cybercrimes due to their particular impact on the economy and consumer health and safety. The United States remains intent on improving the transparency of the international financial system, including an effort to expose vulnerabilities that could be exploited by terrorist and other illicit financial networks. At the same time, the United States will enhance and apply our financial tools and sanctions more effectively to close those vulnerabilities, disrupt and dismantle illicit financial networks, and apply pressure on the state entities that directly or indirectly support TOC. We will continue to monitor TOC infiltration of the global economy to better protect the financial system and freeze the assets of criminal networks under expanded Presidential sanctions authorities and/or seize them under existing forfeiture laws.

### Actions

A. Implement a new Executive Order to prohibit the transactions and block the assets under U.S. jurisdiction of TOC networks and their associates that threaten critical U.S. interests.

B. Prevent or disrupt criminal involvement in emerging and strategic markets.

C. Increase awareness and provide incentives and alternatives for the private sector to reduce facilitation of TOC.

D. Develop a mechanism that would make unclassified data on TOC available to private sector partners.

E. Implement the Administration's joint strategic plan on intellectual property enforcement to target, investigate, and prosecute intellectual property crimes committed by TOC.

F. Enhance domestic and foreign capabilities to combat the increasing involvement of TOC networks in cybercrime and build international capacity to forensically exploit and judicially process digital evidence.

G. Use authorities under the USA PATRIOT Act to designate foreign jurisdictions, institutions, or classes of transactions as "primary money-laundering concerns," allowing for the introduction of various restrictive measures on financial dealings by U.S. persons with those entities.

H. Identify foreign kleptocrats who have corrupt relationships with TOC networks and target their assets for freezing, forfeiture, and repatriation to victimized governments.

I. Work with Congress to enact legislation to require disclosure of beneficial ownership information of legal entities at the time of company formation in order to enhance transparency for law enforcement and other purposes.

J. Support the work of the Financial Action Task Force, which sets and enforces global standards to combat both money laundering and the financing of terrorism.

---

### The Mogilevich Organization

Semion Mogilevich is wanted by the United States for fraud, racketeering, and money laundering and was recently added to the FBI's Ten Most Wanted fugitives list. Mogilevich and several members of his criminal organization were charged in 2003 in the Eastern District of Pennsylvania in a 45-count racketeering indictment with involvement in a sophisticated securities fraud and money-laundering scheme, in which they allegedly used a Pennsylvania company, YBM Magnex, to defraud investors of more than $150 million. Even after that indictment—and being placed on the FBI's Ten Most Wanted list—Mogilevich has continued to expand his criminal empire. Mogilevich was arrested by Russian police on tax charges in January 2008 and was released pending trial in July 2009. Other members of his organization remain at large.

## Strengthen Interdiction, Investigations, and Prosecutions

This *Strategy* sets priorities and objectives to help law enforcement and other applicable agencies at the Federal, State, local, territorial and tribal levels work together in a collaborative manner to target TOC networks—their leaders as well as their enabling means and infrastructure—in the United States and abroad. It is equally important that we build strong working relationships with our international partners to harmonize our efforts, and to ensure that they have the capabilities and regulatory and legislative frameworks to prevent, reduce, and eliminate TOC threats.

Building upon the improved information sharing described earlier, the United States will leverage consolidated TOC databases to provide more accurate intelligence on known TOC members and their associates so they can more easily be denied entry to the United States or access to lawful immigration status, employment, or secure facilities.

This *Strategy* pursues TOC through criminal investigations and interdiction focused on both the networks and their leadership. Criminal investigations will use an integrated approach that incorporates financial, weapons, and TOC-related corruption investigations into a comprehensive attack on the entire criminal organization. Interdiction efforts will focus on depriving TOC networks of their products, proceeds, infrastructure, and enabling means. The use of multi-agency task forces such as the ICE-led Border Enforcement Security Task Forces will remain essential to our efforts to investigate and interdict TOC threats at our borders.

To address recent TOC trends, the Administration will work with Congress on a range of legislative solutions to allow or enhance the prosecution of TOC enterprises and significant TOC activity that affects the United States. We will also enhance our anti-money laundering and forfeiture authorities to target TOC networks that pose threats to national and international security.

### Actions

A.  Work with Congress to enhance U.S. authorities to identify, investigate, interdict, and prosecute top transnational criminal networks.

B.  Utilize rewards programs to assist in gathering information leading to the arrest or conviction of top transnational criminals.

C.  Issue a new Presidential Proclamation under the Immigration and Nationality Act to refuse visas/ deny entry to TOC-affiliated aliens, corrupt foreign officials, and other persons designated for financial sanctions pursuant to the International Emergency Economic Powers Act.

D.  Develop a strategy that denies TOC networks and individuals in the United States access to their infrastructure and their enabling means.

E.  Deny visas to TOC members and associates and capture top TOC figures who take refuge in the United States or partner countries.

F.  Fully integrate financial, weapons, and TOC-related corruption investigations into comprehensive organizational attack activities and operations.

G.  Strengthen cooperation with international police organizations, such as Interpol, Europol, Ameripol, and the International Association of Chiefs of Police (IACP), to facilitate cross-border police cooperation.

H.  Strengthen efforts to interdict illicit trafficking in the air and maritime domains.

I.  Develop and implement a whole-of-government plan to counter kidnapping for ransom in order to disrupt the funding for terrorists, pirates, and other bad actors.

J.  Deny TOC access to secure facilities and locations.

---

### The U.S. Secret Service's Cyber Intelligence Efforts

The U.S. Secret Service leverages technology and information obtained through private partnerships to monitor developing technologies and trends in the financial payments industry. The information obtained is used to enhance the U.S. Secret Service's capabilities to prevent and mitigate attacks against the financial and telecommunications infrastructures. This approach to intelligence collection and sharing has resulted in the successful apprehension of individuals charged with committing some of the world's most advanced cybercrimes during such investigations as those of the Heartland and TJX Intrusions, Maksym Yastremskey, Albert Gonzalez, and others. In FY 2010, the U.S. Secret Service arrested 1,217 suspects for cybercrime related violations, with a fraud loss of $507 million.

### Defending U.S. Borders against TOC

In 2006, amidst rising crime on the Southwest border, ICE and CBP worked with other Federal, State, local, and foreign partners to establish the Border Enforcement Security Task Force (BEST), designed to attack TOC networks that exploit our borders and threaten the American public. Since then, this initiative has grown to 21 BESTs arrayed along the Southwest and Northern borders as well as at major seaports. These BESTs have seized more than 36,000 pounds of cocaine, 550 pounds of heroin, 485,000 pounds of marijuana, 4,300 weapons, and $68 million, and led to the arrests of 5,910 individuals.

## Disrupt Drug Trafficking and Its Facilitation of Other Transnational Threats

In recent years, new developments in technology and communications equipment have enabled TOC networks involved in drug trafficking and other illicit activities to plan, coordinate, and perpetrate their schemes with increased mobility and anonymity. As a result, many DTOs have developed into versatile, loose networks that cooperate intermittently but maintain their independence. They operate worldwide and employ sophisticated technology and financial savvy. These criminal networks bribe government officials and take advantage of weak border security and ill-equipped law enforcement to facilitate their operations. Along emerging trafficking routes, such as the transit route through West Africa to Europe, criminal networks are spreading corruption and undermining fledgling democratic institutions. Due to the enormous profits associated with drug trafficking, the illegal trade is also a way to finance other transnational criminal and terrorist activities.

To diminish these threats, we will continue ongoing efforts to identify and disrupt the leadership, production, intelligence gathering, transportation, and financial infrastructure of major TOC networks. By targeting the human, technology, travel, and communications aspects of these networks, we will be able to monitor and gather intelligence to identify the full scope of the TOC networks, their members, financial assets, and criminal activities. We will continue ongoing efforts to enhance collaboration among domestic law enforcement agencies and our foreign counterparts in order to strengthen our ability to coordinate investigations and share intelligence to combat drug trafficking and TOC. Continued use of economic sanctions under the Foreign Narcotics Kingpin Designation Act (Kingpin Act) to pursue transnational drug organizations will enhance our ability to disrupt and dismantle TOC networks. The Kingpin Act also may be used to prosecute persons involved in illegal activities linked to drug trafficking, such as arms trafficking, bulk cash smuggling, or gang activity. Enhanced intelligence sharing and coordination among law enforcement and intelligence agencies, the military, and our diplomatic community will enable the interagency community to develop aggressive, multi-jurisdictional approaches to dismantle TOC networks involved in drug trafficking.

The United States will continue to aggressively target the nexus among TOC networks involved in drug trafficking, terrorist groups, piracy on the high seas, and arms traffickers. In FY 2002, the DEA formally established the Counter-Narco-Terrorism Operations Center (CNTOC) within SOD, which coordinates all DEA investigations and intelligence linked to narco-terrorism and is central to U.S. efforts to disrupt these crime-terror relationships. The United States will utilize its bilateral maritime counterdrug agreements and operational procedures to facilitate cooperation in counterdrug operations. We must attack these organizations as close to the source as we can by forward deploying our law enforcement and intelligence assets. All-source intelligence is used by U.S. Coast Guard assets in the transit zone to extend our borders by interdicting and apprehending traffickers.

The United States will continue its longstanding cooperation with the international community in our joint efforts to disrupt the world drug trade through support for drug crop reduction, promotion of alternative livelihoods, and partner nation capacity building. Our counternarcotics efforts will apply all available tools to ensure that improvements are permanent and sustainable by international allies. These efforts will include complementary and comprehensive assistance programs across the prevention, intervention, and enforcement spectrum. By disrupting and dismantling the world's major TOC networks involved in drug trafficking, we will be able to reduce the availability of illicit drugs, inhibit terrorist funding, improve national and international security, and bring TOC networks to justice.

## Actions

A. Work with international partners to reduce the global supply of and demand for illegal drugs and thereby deny funding to TOC networks.

B. Sever the links between the international illicit drug and arms trades, especially in strategic regions that are at risk of being destabilized by these interconnected threats.

C. Sustain pressure to disrupt Consolidated Priority Organization Targets, as they often have a particularly corrupting influence or provide support to terrorism.

D. Maximize use of the Kingpin Act to pursue transnational drug organizations.

E. Develop a comprehensive approach to dismantle DTOs with connections to terrorist organizations.

F. Work with international partners to shut down emerging drug transit routes and associated corruption in West Africa.

G. Coordinate with international partners to prevent synthetic drug production, trafficking, and precursor chemical diversion.

### Countering Illicit Finance for Drug Traffickers & Terrorists

In February 2011, the U.S. Department of the Treasury, based upon an investigation by the DEA, announced the identification of the Lebanese Canadian Bank (LCB) as a financial institution of primary money laundering concern under Section 311 of the USA PATRIOT Act. The Department of the Treasury found there was reason to believe LCB managers were complicit in facilitating the money-laundering activities of an international narcotics trafficking and money laundering network controlled by Ayman Joumaa who was designated as a drug Kingpin on January 26, 2011 pursuant to the Kingpin Act. This network moved illegal drugs from South America to Europe and the Middle East via West Africa and laundered hundreds of millions of dollars monthly through accounts held at LCB, as well as through trade-based money laundering involving consumer goods throughout the world, including through used car dealerships in the United States. The U.S. Government also found reason to believe there were links between the international narcotics trafficking and money laundering network, LCB, and the terrorist organization Hizballah.

### International Drug Enforcement Conference

The annual DEA-led International Drug Enforcement Conference (IDEC), which has been held annually for the past 28 years, is a major contributor to international cooperation and capacity building. The IDEC brings the top drug law enforcement leaders and senior investigators from over 100 nations to a single venue where yearly agendas are set for cooperation, intelligence sharing, and case prioritization. IDEC—the world's largest international drug law enforcement conference—has produced concrete results year after year. During the conferences, DEA and partner nations jointly develop plans to build greater law enforcement and investigatory capacity. In addition, host nation personnel and U.S. law enforcement exchange information on priority investigatory targets.

## Build International Capacity, Cooperation, and Partnerships

Sustainable progress against TOC requires both political commitment and effective law enforcement and criminal justice capacities on a worldwide basis. TOC threatens the security and well-being of people around the world and jeopardizes the functioning of the global economy. Not all of these threats are equally visible to international audiences. Absent broad recognition of these shared threats, our collaboration with international partners to confront TOC will be constrained by limited political will. The United States will reach out directly to the international business community and the general public to convey that both nations and individuals share a common enemy in TOC and have a common stake in addressing this threat.

For nations that have the will to fulfill their international law enforcement commitments but lack the necessary means, the United States is committed to partnering with them to develop stronger law enforcement and criminal justice institutions necessary for ensuring the rule of law. Over the past decade, important gains have been made in developing criminal justice capacities in key regions of the world. The goal of the United States is to promote the expansion of such achievements on a worldwide basis, to the point where international law enforcement capabilities and cooperation among states are self-sustaining. Great progress also has been made in developing a common normative framework for international cooperation against TOC threats. The challenge for the United States and other countries over the next decade is to bring the promise of this worldwide regime into practice. The United States will encourage international partners to dedicate the necessary political capital and resources toward making the promise of these commitments a reality. The United States will pursue this through both a renewed commitment to multilateral diplomacy and by leveraging bilateral partnerships to elevate the importance of combating TOC as a key priority of U.S. diplomacy. For example, in February 2011, the United States and the United Kingdom established the Organized Crime Contact Group, to be chaired by the UK Home Secretary and the Assistant to the President for Homeland Security and Counterterrorism. In addition, the United States deploys hundreds of law enforcement attachés to its missions abroad to develop and maintain foreign contacts essential to combating immediate threats to public safety and security. The United States will continue to place a high priority on the provision of international technical assistance through our missions abroad and will continue to improve the coordination of these programs.

The United States will leverage all possible areas of cooperation, including legal instruments such as the *UN Convention against Transnational Organized Crime (the Palermo Convention),* the *UN Convention against the Illicit Traffic in Narcotic Drugs and Psychotropic Substances,* and the protocols to which the United States is a party, to obtain the assistance of international partners and to raise international criminal justice, border security, and law enforcement standards and norms. The United States will strengthen its engagement with the United Nations in this regard and leverage the growing role of regional and other multilateral institutions that have risen in significance and influence over the past decade. Additionally, the United States will continue to pursue cooperation with other countries and with partners such as the European Union, the G-8, the G-20, and new inter-regional platforms across the Pacific and Atlantic in developing leading-edge initiatives and political commitments to combat TOC.

The United States also will seek to develop informal partnerships with states that share U.S. goals to prevent TOC networks from abusing the benefits of globalization. By promoting flexible networks of law enforcement and diplomatic partners, the United States can leverage the expertise and infrastructure of committed governments and respond more quickly to changing dynamics in transnational criminal threats. The United States convened a meeting of 25 countries and jurisdictions across the Pacific in April 2009 to consider common approaches and strengthen cooperation against transnational criminal networks that span East Asia, the Pacific, and Latin America. The United States hosted a similar event in May 2011 with the European Union to generate enhanced partnerships against trans-Atlantic criminal networks operating across Latin America, West Africa, and Europe. By building cooperative platforms and networks incrementally, the United States will generate greater collective action, joint cases, and common strategic approaches with our international partners to combat transnational criminal threats.

## Actions

A.  Raise international awareness of TOC and build multilateral cooperation against it.

B.  Partner with countries able to contribute key law enforcement resources, other donors, and the United Nations to launch a new International Police Peacekeeping Operations Support Program to enhance policing and law enforcement capacity in ungoverned spaces.

C.  Leverage assets to enhance foreign capabilities, including counterterrorism capacity building, foreign law enforcement cooperation, military cooperation, and the strengthening of justice and interior ministries.

D.  Implement a public diplomacy strategy to reduce the demand for illicit goods and services that fuels TOC.

E.  Implement the Central American Citizen Security Partnership to strengthen courts, civil society groups and institutions that uphold the rule of law in the region.

F.  Implement the State Department's West Africa Citizen Security Initiative to combat transnational criminal threats in the region.

G.  Initiate new dialogue in multilateral fora to combat corruption and illicit trade, to include, as part of the Administration's intellectual property enforcement strategy, stemming the flow of dangerous counterfeit products.

H.  Build partnerships with other donors, private sector experts, nongovernmental organizations, civil society groups, the media, and academia that focus on supporting political will for criminal justice reform.

I.  Increase international scientific research, data collection, and analysis to assess the scope and impact of TOC and the most effective means to combat it.

J.  Institutionalize the U.S.-UK Organized Crime Contact Group to deepen bilateral cooperation and galvanize multilateral collaboration against TOC.

K.  Finalize the U.S.-Mexico 21st Century Border Action Plan agreements on law enforcement cooperation.

L.  Expand cooperation with the United Nations to promote implementation of the United Nations Convention against Transnational Organized Crime, including through the development of an appropriate review mechanism.

M. Strengthen capacities for program management, internal controls, and contract administration to prevent the diversion or improper use of foreign assistance in countries threatened by TOC-related corruption.

N. Increase collaboration with international partners to improve their capacity to support immigration, customs, transportation, and critical infrastructure screening requirements and to harmonize their standards for screening and identification.

---

### Combating Transnational Crime: The Multilateral Framework

Five major international agreements underpin and provide near global scope to our efforts to combat TOC and corruption: the United Nations Convention against Transnational Organized Crime (UNTOC), its three supplementary protocols against trafficking in persons, migrant smuggling, and illicit trafficking in firearms, and the United Nations Convention against Corruption (UNCAC). The United States strongly supports the framework provided by these instruments, especially with regard to prosecuting and investigating transnational crime and corruption, engaging in mutual legal assistance, and supplementing bilateral extradition treaties. These agreements set the point of departure for many of our bilateral law enforcement partnerships around the globe and help bring the international community into agreement with U.S. standards. The key challenge remaining is to promote wider implementation of the Conventions through support for capacity building and by otherwise encouraging international partners to dedicate the necessary political capital and resources toward realizing the potential of these groundbreaking instruments.

www.ingramcontent.com/pod-product-compliance
Lightning Source LLC
Chambersburg PA
CBHW080734290526
45790CB00008B/3195